FURTHER INFORMATION

Books

Currie, Stephen. *Australia and the Pacific Islands* (Exploration and Discovery). Lucent Books, 2004.

Day, Alan. *The A to Z of the Discovery and Exploration of Australia* (A to Z Guide series). Scarecrow Press, 2009.

Explorers: Great Tales of Adventure and Endurance. DK Publishing, 2010.

Feinstein, Stephen. *Captain Cook: Great Explorer of the Pacific* (Great Explorers of the World). Enslow Publishers, 2010.

Morriss, Roger. *Captain Cook and his Exploration of the Pacific* (History of Exploration). Newforest Press, 2010.

Vail, Martha. *Exploring the Pacific* (Discovery and Exploration). Chelsea House Publications, 2009.

Websites

http://www.abc.net.au/navigators/history/default.htm
Australian Broadcasting Corporation history of exploration in Australia.

http://www.teara.govt.nz/en/european-exploration
Article on exploration from the government-sponsored online Encyclopedia of New Zealand.

http://www.rmg.co.uk/explore/sea-and-ships/cook
Greenwich Maritime Museum pages about James Cook.

Publisher's note to educators and parents: Our editors have carefully reviewed these websites to ensure that they are suitable for students. Many websites change frequently, however, and we cannot guarantee that a site's future contents will continue to meet our high standards of quality and educational value. Be advised that students should be closely supervised whenever they access the Internet.

INDEX

EXPLORERS DISCOVERING THE WORLD

THE EXPLORATION OF AUSTRALASIA AND THE PACIFIC

Tim Cooke

Gareth Stevens
Publishing

Please visit our website, www.garethstevens.com. For a free color catalog of all our high-quality books, call toll-free 1-800-542-2595 or fax 1-877-542-2596.

Library of Congress Cataloging-in-Publication Data

Cooke, Tim.
 The exploration of Australasia and the Pacific / Tim Cooke.
    p. cm. — (Explorers discovering the world)
 Includes index.
ISBN 978-1-4339-8620-8 (pbk.)
ISBN 978-1-4339-8621-5 (6-pack)
ISBN 978-1-4339-8619-2 (library binding)
1. Australasia—Discovery and exploration—Juvenile literature. 2. Pacific Islands—Discovery and explora-
tion—Juvenile literature. I. Title.
 DU98.1.C76 2013
 919—dc23

2012037757

ISBN 978-1-4339-8620-8 (pbk.)
ISBN 978-1-4339-8621-5 (6-pack)
ISBN 978-1-4339-8619-2 (library binding)

Published in 2013 by
Gareth Stevens Publishing
111 East 14th Street, Suite 349
New York, NY 10003

© 2013 Brown Bear Books Ltd

For Brown Bear Books Ltd:
Editorial Director: Lindsey Lowe
Managing Editor: Tim Cooke
Children's Publisher: Anne O'Daly
Art Director: Jeni Child
Designer: Lynne Lennon
Picture Manager: Sophie Mortimer

Manufactured in the United States of America
1 2 3 4 5 6 7 8 9 12 11 10

CPSIA compliance information: Batch #CW13GS. For further information contact Gareth Stevens, New York, New York at 1-800-542-2595.

CONTENTS

INTRODUCTION

In the 17th and 18th centuries, European governments sent explorers into the Pacific Ocean to seek new trade routes to east Asia and the Spice Islands. The improvement of scientific instruments in the 18th century led to a surge in the accurate charting of the Pacific and its numerous islands.

Many of the original exploratory and surveying expeditions took scientists and naturalists along. They recorded and collected many thousands of previously unknown animal and plant species.

Inland Australia

It was only at the end of the 18th century that Europeans confirmed that Australia was a vast continent. But its interior remained uncharted and inhospitable, known only to the native Aborigines. Within less than 50 years, however, much of the country had been explored, surveyed, and mapped. In neighboring New Zealand, meanwhile, missionaries led the way in exploring the wild countryside.

An aboriginal painting of a turtle: some European explorers learned survival techniques from friendly native Aborigines.

The Australian Outback has a strange beauty, but the baking deserts and scrub were an inhospitable landscape for explorers where water was scarce.

1605–1643

ABEL TASMAN AND THE DUTCH

Abel Tasman worked for the Dutch East India Company. He captained a ship sailing between Europe and the Spice Islands of what is now Indonesia. In 1642, the East India Company sent him to find out about New Holland, as the Dutch called Australia.

Willem Jansz was the first European to see Australia, in 1605. He thought it was an island, however, and didn't realize it was large enough to be a continent.

DID YOU KNOW?

The Dutch East India Company was formed in 1602 to trade with the Spice Islands in the Indian Ocean.

Batavia, on the island of Java in Indonesia, was the capital of the Dutch East Indies and the base for the Dutch exploration of Australasia.

Tasman sailed from Batavia (modern-day Jakarta) in Indonesia. He first sailed west into the Indian Ocean. There he caught the westerly winds that helped ships sail around the tip of Africa. The winds pushed him southeast, toward New Holland.

Too Far South

Tasman's course took him so far south he missed Australia. As he got near Antarctica, his crew complained of being too cold. Tasman headed north—but again failed to reach Australia. He did see one island, which he claimed for the Netherlands. It was later named Tasmania for him.

WILLEM JANSZ

The Dutch had first reached Australia in 1605. Willem Jansz was sent from Java by the Dutch East India Company to find new lands. On his return, he reported seeing a large tropical island to the south. This was an understatement. Jansz had passed the northeast coast of Australia. He was the first European to locate the new continent: he just didn't know it!

1605–1643

Tasman sailed east from Tasmania for nine days. He saw land, but had to sail for three more days until he found somewhere safe to dock. This was Golden Bay, the most northern point of what is now the South Island of New Zealand.

Hostile Welcome

There were signs that people were living along the coast. As Tasman's officers rowed ashore, however, Maori warriors suddenly appeared in war canoes. They attacked the boat and killed four Dutch officers. Tasman sailed away.

DID YOU KNOW?

Tasman named Golden Bay Murderers' Bay after the Maori warriors had killed his officers there.

Cape Farewell in New Zealand was discovered by Abel Tasman in 1642; it was named by James Cook in 1770, as his crew sailed away from New Zealand.

Sheldon Lagoon is on Cape York in Australia; most of the Dutch seafarers did not land, so they had no idea what inland Australia was like.

THE SPICE TRADE

Spices were very valuable in Europe: they helped disguise the taste of bland or old food. The Dutch were eager to have a share of the lucrative trade. In 1619, the Dutch East India Company set up its headquarters in Batavia— now Jakarta, Indonesia. From there, ships carried spices back to Europe. The Dutch also founded Cape Colony in southern Africa as a stopping place for ships heading to and from the East Indies.

Safety First

Tasman reached Batavia in June 1643. He made a second journey six months later. This time, he sailed south of New Guinea and then into the Gulf of Carpentaria. He sailed along the Australian coast but did not stop to explore it. Historians later criticized the decision not to land. After the murders in New Zealand, however, Tasman's priority was to keep his ships and crew safe.

Cinnamon had been imported from Asia and Africa to Europe since biblical times to give its spicy flavor to food and drinks.

1616–1740

PACIFIC VOYAGES

In the 17th and 18th centuries, Dutch and English sailors charted new territory across the Pacific Ocean. The Dutch wanted to sail to Asia via the Strait of Magellan, at the tip of South America. In 1616, Willem Schouten missed the strait and accidentally found Cape Horn, the southern tip of the Americas.

The Pacific Islands were home to rich vegetation that the Europeans had never seen before; but the vegetation sometimes hid a hostile reception.

This 1726 illustration shows a Dutch ship in New Guinea, which had been discovered by Portuguese and Spanish sailors but was later claimed by the Dutch.

ALEXANDER SELKIRK

Scottish sailor Alexander Selkirk was marooned on Juan Fernandez Island in the Pacific after a row with his captain. He lived on the island for four years until Dampier's ship spotted a fire signal in 1709. Selkirk was like a wild man, wearing goatskins and barely able to speak English. He inspired the novel Robinson Crusoe.

English explorers also crossed the Pacific. They included William Adams, who reached Japan, and William Dampier, who landed on Australia's northwest coast in 1688. In 1697, Dampier returned to Australia. This time, he ended up on the west coast.

English Circumnavigation

In 1740, the Royal Navy admiral George Anson was sent to the Pacific to attack Spanish territories. The mission was a disaster, but Anson sailed west. He eventually reached home, having sailed around the world.

1768–1779

JAMES COOK

Cook and his officers are honored by native people on the Sandwich Islands, now Etafe in the Republic of Vanuatu in the Pacific.

Captain James Cook is one of the most famous of all explorers. On three separate voyages, he mapped much of the world and claimed new territory for Britain, including Australia. He made his first voyage in 1768. He was sent to Tahiti in the Pacific Ocean to observe the transit of the planet Venus across the front of the sun.

Cook was also told to search for the Great Southern Continent, Terra Australis.

Sailing South

Cook sailed for the Pacific on the HMS *Endeavour* with naturalists and an astronomer. They arrived in Tahiti on April 13, 1769, and received a friendly welcome. After the scientists had observed the transit of Venus, the *Endeavour* sailed on to New Zealand. Cook charted the coastline of the islands but did not attempt to explore because of the fierce appearance of the native Maori.

Cook used traditional tools like this sextant for navigation. He also used the chronometer, a brand-new device that kept accurate time at sea.

James Cook charted huge areas, including much of New Zealand, the east coast of Australia, many remote islands, and the Antarctic.

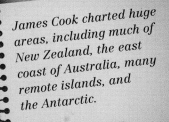

TERRA AUSTRALIS

For centuries, maps showed an imaginary Terra Australis, or "southern land." People thought that Europe, Asia, and North America must be balanced by a large continent in the Southern Hemisphere. On Cook's second voyage (1772– 1775), he sailed around the globe near the Antarctic Circle. He showed that, if Terra Australis existed, it was icy and uninhabited.

DID YOU KNOW?

Cook was such an expert navigator that he could tell by the swell of the sea whether or not the ship was near land.

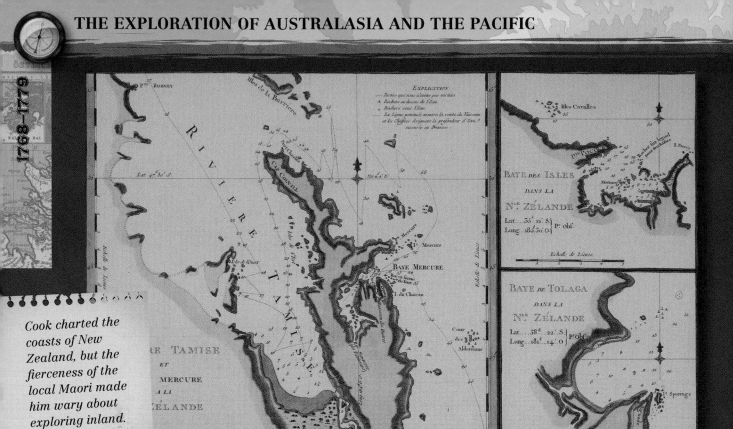

Cook charted the coasts of New Zealand, but the fierceness of the local Maori made him wary about exploring inland.

Cook set out for Tasmania but was blown off course. Instead he landed on the Australian mainland. On April 19, 1770, Cook sailed into Botany Bay and raised the British flag. Cook continued sailing up the east coast of Australia. As he explored the Great Barrier Reef, the *Endeavour* was almost lost when it ran onto the coral. On the way home, Cook lost a third of his crew to scurvy.

Second Voyage

On his second voyage, Cook headed south in search of Terra Australis. In January 1774, Cook's ship *Resolution* reached further south than anyone before him. But icebergs prevented him reaching the coast of Antarctica. He sailed home via the South Pacific, visiting Easter Island, Tahiti, the New Hebrides, and New Caledonia.

DID YOU KNOW?

Cook named Botany Bay because his scientists were able to collect so many plant specimens there.

From 1795, the Royal Navy used lemon and lime juice to give sailors the vitamin C they needed to avoid getting scurvy.

Final Voyage

Cook's third journey aimed to find the Pacific entrance to the Northwest Passage, a route around the top of North America. He sailed to New Zealand in early 1777, then across the Pacific to Alaska and the Arctic Ocean. He then sailed back to Hawaii, which he had sighted on the voyage north. But he was killed during an argument with some natives who were trying to steal a boat. His deputy, Charles Clerke, took Cook's ship, *Resolution*, back to Britain.

SCURVY

At sea, sailors who ate only salted meat and dried biscuits suffered from scurvy, a disease caused by a lack of vitamin C. Cook made sure that his crew ate fresh fruit and vegetables, which were known to prevent scurvy. In 1754, James Lind suggested that sailors should drink lemon or lime juice. Cases of scurvy fell sharply.

On Hawaii, Cook originally received a warm welcome from the local people, but later tension developed that would lead to his death in 1779.

1766–1769

LOUIS DE BOUGAINVILLE

The French were Britain's great rivals in the Pacific. They wanted the same kind of success as Captain Cook, especially after they lost their North American colony, Louisiana, to Spain. Bougainville hoped to discover a new French empire. In 1766, he sailed from France on a new warship, the *Boudeuse*.

Bougainville's destination, Mauritius, had been a French colony since 1715, when France took it from the Dutch. Its economy was based on growing and trading sugar cane.

DID YOU KNOW?

Bougainville's astronomer, Pierre-Antoine Véron, made the first accurate measurement of the width of the Pacific.

The cloves and nutmeg Bougainville intended to plant in Mauritius may have died on the voyage—or he may simply have forgotten to load them.

LATITUDE AND LONGITUDE

Latitude and longitude refer to imaginary lines that run around the globe from east to west and from north to south, respectively. They are used by navigators to chart their location. Positions are expressed in terms of degrees and minutes relative to the equator (0 degrees latitude) or the Greenwich meridian (0 degrees longitude).

Bougainville reached the Pacific via South America. Although many of his sailors suffered from scurvy, he sailed across the Pacific. He discovered the Louisiades Islands and measured how wide the ocean was.

A Failed Trip

The *Boudeuse* finally reached the island of Mauritius. Bougainville was meant to bring plants from the Spice Islands so that the French colony could grow its own spices. The plants may have died, because none were planted. Bougainville sailed for home and arrived in France in March 1769. His journey had not been a success—but it had taken him around the globe.

Bougainville receives a warm welcome in Tahiti in April 1768. The Tahitians helped the French sailors recover from scurvy.

1785–1788

JEAN-FRANÇOIS DE LA PÉROUSE

A French nobleman, La Pérouse was chosen in 1785 to lead the most expensive expedition ever. His ships, *Astrolabe* and *Boussole*, had the very latest scientific equipment on board. Their mission was to restore the French national reputation and give France a lead in scientific research.

La Pérouse visited Easter Island, where he studied the moai, carved statues of ancestors set up by ancient islanders to look over the island.

DID YOU KNOW?

By the time La Pérouse was ordered to sail to Botany Bay, the British had already turned it into a prison colony.

Jean-François de Galaup, count of La Pérouse, was sent on his expedition by King Louis XVI of France.

La Pérouse sailed around Cape Horn and up the Chilean coast to Easter Island. Heading north to Alaska, he lost 20 men in rough seas. From Monterey, California, he set off across the Pacific.

What Happened to La Pérouse?

After more than 100 days, the crew saw Macao off the Chinese coast. After spending the winter in Kamchatka, La Pérouse received orders to sail for Botany Bay in Australia. He landed there in January 1788 and set off to map the north coast of Australia. Neither ship was ever seen again.

CHRONOMETER

Calculating longitude depended on knowing the precise time. But no clock kept accurate time on a rocking ship. In 1714, a huge reward—$2 million today—was offered for a clock that kept accurate time at sea. John Harrison, a self-taught engineer, won the prize with his chronometer. His fourth version of the device, the H-4, lost only seconds during 81 days at sea.

1791–1793

ANTOINE D'ENTRECASTEAUX

In 1791, three years after La Pérouse disappeared, the French sent a naval officer to look for him. Antoine d'Entrecasteaux set sail with two ships. He planned to sail to the west coast of Australia from the Cape of Good Hope at the tip of Africa.

This Maori carving shows a tattooed warrior. D'Entrecasteaux sighted New Zealand, but did not land there.

DID YOU KNOW?

D'Entrecasteaux's officers and crew supported different sides in the French Revolution. That caused bitter rows.

Pitcairn Island is still home to the descendants of Fletcher Christian and the other mutineers from the HMS Bounty.

In South Africa, d'Entrecasteaux heard a rumor that La Pérouse was in the Admiralty Islands. He changed course and headed there via southern Australia and Tasmania, sighting New Zealand on the way. There was no sign of La Pérouse.

News from Home

After two years at sea, the expedition reached Amboina in the South China Sea in September 1792. D'Entrecasteaux turned for home, visiting more of the Pacific Islands on the way. He died from scurvy on July 29, 1793. The new captain who took over eventually surrendered the ship to the Dutch authorities in South Africa.

MUTINY ON THE *BOUNTY*

The HMS Bounty *was sent to the Pacific in 1789 to collect breadfruit to take to Britain's Caribbean colonies. The captain, William Bligh, was hated by the crew. The first mate, Fletcher Christian, led a mutiny. The crew set Bligh and a few loyal sailors adrift in an open boat. They survived and made it home. The mutineers settled on Pitcairn Island in the South Pacific.*

1778–1792

GEORGE VANCOUVER

Vancouver joined the navy at age 13 and sailed with James Cook. This statue stands in his birthplace, King's Lynn, in eastern England.

Not all the Pacific is tropical islands. George Vancouver is famous for his association with the cooler Pacific Northwest. The British navy sent him to explore the Pacific in April 1791, collecting botanical samples and surveying coastlines. Vancouver sailed to Cape Town, then on to Australia, New Zealand, Tahiti, and China.

DID YOU KNOW?

Vancouver's ships, *Discovery* and *Chatham*, traveled 65,244 miles (105,000 km) on the trip from 1791 to 1795.

Vancouver discovered the chilly San Juan Islands north of the strait of Juan de Fuca, between Vancouver Island and the North American mainland.

Vancouver crossed the northern Pacific and sailed up the coasts of Oregon and Washington. On April 29, 1792, he entered the strait between what is now Vancouver Island and the mainland.

Mapping British Colombia

Vancouver had visited the west coast of North America on Captain Cook's third voyage in 1778, but bad weather stopped the crew from seeing much. This time, he made detailed charts of the coast between California and Alaska. In all, he charted 16,777 miles (27,000 km) of coastline. His maps were so detailed they were not improved on for 100 years.

THE FAR NORTH

Another explorer in the northern Pacific was Alessandro Malaspina, an Italian in the Spanish navy. From 1789 to 1794, he charted what he called "the most remote region of America." He took scientists and artists who studied the Tlingit people of the Pacific Northwest. Malaspina charted the coasts of Washington, California, and Oregon.

1788–1808

NEW SOUTH WALES

The British were attracted to the New South Wales coast by its natural harbors, including what is now Sydney Harbor.

The British created a penal colony in New South Wales, in southeastern Australia. The first six transport ships docked at Port Jackson (now Sydney) in January 1788. On board was the first governor of Australia, Arthur Phillips, together with 730 convicts: 570 men and 160 women.

The First Fleet also brought sailors, livestock, and supplies to start the colony. Many of the new arrivals were sick after the eight-month voyage. But as soon as they landed, convicts and sailors both set to work to build shelters and hunt for food.

Convict Life

It was two and a half years before relief ships arrived. By then, the settlers were near starvation. They had cleared land to farm, but farming methods from home didn't work in the hot climate. It was difficult to grow food. It was another 20 years before colonists dared travel inland.

PORT JACKSON

Arthur Phillips chose Port Jackson as a better site for settlement than Botany Bay. Conditions were hard and discipline was harsh. The first job of the convicts was to build shelters. They were originally wooden, but were later replaced by stone structures. When food proved more difficult to grow than expected, the settlers were forced to try to catch fish and to hunt kangaroos for meat.

Arthur Phillips (center) founds Port Jackson in this bronze plaque from the colony's modern equivalent, Sydney.

1798–1810

MATTHEW FLINDERS

Royal Navy captain Matthew Flinders was the first person to sail around Australia and confirm that it was a continent. He arrived in Australia aged just 21. With George Bass, he explored the coast on a small sailing boat. The pair were sent on a larger ship to find out if Tasmania was an island.

On the way home from Australia, Flinders was arrested on Mauritius by the French, with whom Britain was at war. He only arrived back in Britain in 1810.

DID YOU KNOW?

Flinders' ship, the *Investigator*, leaked so badly he gave up charting the coast and speeded up his voyage to avoid sinking.

In September 1798, Flinders and his crew of eight sailed through what was later named Bass Strait, for his fellow explorer. It was clear that Tasmania was indeed an island.

A Bigger Circumnavigation

Now Flinders was ordered to try to sail around Australia. He started at Cape Leeuwin, on the southwestern tip, in 1801. He sailed east, meeting the French explorer Nicolas Baudin. As Flinders went on, his boat began leaking. Still, he managed to sail on around the continent, completing the circumnavigation before landing at Sydney in June 1803.

Sea lions confront one another on Kangaroo Island. Flinders discovered and named the island, which he explored at the same time as Nicolas Baudin.

NICHOLAS BAUDIN

Nicholas Baudin was captain of the French warship Geographe. *In 1800, the new emperor of France, Napoleon, sent him to try to take control of Tasmania. Baudin was also meant to chart the west and north coasts of Australia. But Baudin died during his task in 1803. Much of his work was taken from maps given to him by the English explorer Matthew Flinders.*

1827–1845

CHARLES STURT

Charles Sturt was a pioneer of inland exploration in Australia. He arrived on the continent in 1827 as a soldier. Next year, he set off on his first expedition accompanied by Hamilton Hume, who had been born in Australia. Together, the pair produced maps notable for their great accuracy.

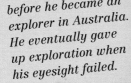

Charles Sturt had been a British soldier before he became an explorer in Australia. He eventually gave up exploration when his eyesight failed.

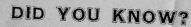

DID YOU KNOW?

Billabong is an Aboriginal word for pond. Australia's ponds, like the Macquarie Marshes, dry up in the summer.

The Great Dividing Range is one of the longest mountain ranges in the world. It runs down eastern Australia, cutting off the coast from the interior.

Sturt and Hume headed to the Great Dividing Range, mountains that cut the east coast off from the rest of the continent. They wanted to discover if rivers running west from the mountains ever reached the ocean. Or did they flow into an inland sea in the unknown center of the country?

A Harsh Journey

Following the route of John Oxley, Sturt and Hume reached the Macquarie Marshes. Rather than the wetland they expected, they found a vast, dry region. The men continued into the Outback and discovered a salty river they named the Darling.

JOHN OXLEY

John Oxley was surveyor-general of New South Wales. In 1818, he headed inland. After 200 miles (320 km), he reached what he named the Macquarie Marshes. Unable to pass the marsh, he crossed the Great Dividing Range east to the Liverpool Plains, which became a cattle-rearing region. Oxley also surveyed Moreton Bay, which is now Brisbane.

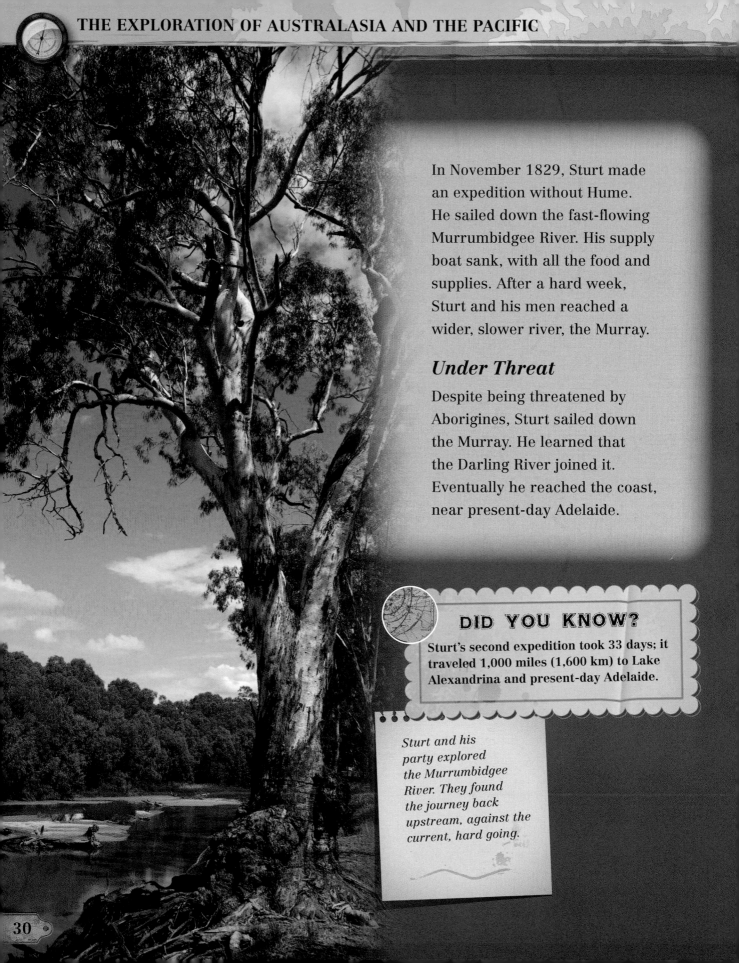

In November 1829, Sturt made an expedition without Hume. He sailed down the fast-flowing Murrumbidgee River. His supply boat sank, with all the food and supplies. After a hard week, Sturt and his men reached a wider, slower river, the Murray.

Under Threat

Despite being threatened by Aborigines, Sturt sailed down the Murray. He learned that the Darling River joined it. Eventually he reached the coast, near present-day Adelaide.

DID YOU KNOW?

Sturt's second expedition took 33 days; it traveled 1,000 miles (1,600 km) to Lake Alexandrina and present-day Adelaide.

Sturt and his party explored the Murrumbidgee River. They found the journey back upstream, against the current, hard going.

Sturt developed scurvy in the hot center of the continent. He was saved by the expedition surgeon, who led the party back to safety.

Another Expedition

In 1844, Sturt led another expedition, this time from Adelaide. He still believed there was a great inland sea in the middle of the continent. By the time his expedition got to Milparinka in January 1845, it was the middle of summer. Temperatures hit 120°F (49°C). The men continued to Cooper Creek, but it became even hotter. Sturt almost died on the trip across the Stony Desert.

ABORIGINES

The Aborigines arrived in Australia about 60,000 years ago. By the time Europeans arrived in the 18th century, about 300,000 Aborigines lived there. They were skilled at finding food and water in the difficult terrain and coping with hot temperatures and the harsh climate. Some were hostile to the Europeans; others were helpful.

1834–1837

THOMAS MITCHELL AND EDWARD EYRE

Edward Eyre opened a 2,000-mile (3,220-km) route along the southern coast; he later became governor of New Zealand.

Major Thomas Mitchell, surveyor-general of New South Wales, disliked Australia, its settlers, and the Aborigines. In 1835, he followed the Darling River for 300 miles (480 km) inland. Another expedition led him to agree with Sturt's belief that the rivers to the north joined up with the Darling.

DID YOU KNOW?

Eyre's companion, John Baxter, was killed by two Aborigine guides, who stole all the expedition's food.

When it is full, Lake Eyre is the largest lake in Australia, and the water is nearly fresh; for most of the time, however, much of it is dry salt flats.

Mitchell's next journey took him to the south coast. He was surprised to find a good climate and fertile soil near a place he named Port Phillip Bay. His positive report sent settlers flocking to the region. In 1837, the city of Melbourne was founded there.

Western Australia

Englishman Edward Eyre arrived in Australia in 1834 and worked as a cattle drover. He discovered Lake Eyre, a vast seasonal lake. His attempt to open a coastal route to Western Australia almost ended in disaster. Only Eyre and an Aboriginal guide survived after weeks with little food or water. A French whaling ship rescued them.

MERINO SHEEP

Much of inland Australia was ideal for raising sheep. One breed suited the hot, dry climate best: the merino sheep from Spain. Settlers were eager to move into the interior because sheep needed a lot of land. Each sheep required an area equivalent to two football fields to graze. With flocks of more than 10,000 sheep, that needed a lot of land.

1844–1848

FRIEDRICH LEICHHARDT

Leichhardt's goal on his first expedition was Port Essington, 2,500 miles (4,000 km) from the start of the journey in Brisbane.

Friedrich Leichhardt was a German naturalist and a terrible explorer. He prepared badly for his journeys and did not pack the right equipment, such as enough water bottles. He was a poor navigator and kept getting lost. But Leichhardt and his party still managed to reach Northern Australia in December 1845.

DID YOU KNOW?

Leichhardt's first expedition covered 2,500 miles (4,000 km); his food supplies ran out after just 400 miles (640 km).

Leichhard set off from Brisbane in October 1844. He arrived in Port Essington, in the far north of Arnhem Land, 14 months later.

An Unknown End

In December 1846, Leichhardt set out to cross Australia from east to west. But he had too little equipment and fell out with his companions. But he was not put off. In March 1848, he set off again. His party was last seen a month later at the Condamine River. They were never heard from again.

MINERAL WEALTH

Australia is rich in minerals. Within 10 years of the first settlers arriving, coal was discovered in Newcastle, New South Wales. It was mined to be used for fuel. In the 1850s, a gold rush brought prospectors flooding to Australia. Soon the country was producing almost 40 percent of the world's gold. The hunt for minerals—lead, copper, tin, and silver, as well as gold—sent prospectors into Australia's interior to brave its harsh conditions.

Aboriginal artists used Australia's range of minerals to make different colors for their rock paintings, which often showed animals in X-ray form.

1860–1861

BURKE AND WILLS

Christopher Robert Burke was an Irishman who emigrated to Australia in 1853. He was chosen to lead the first expedition across the Australian interior. He was a poor choice, as he got lost easily and often made snap decisions. Burke's deputy was an English surveyor, William Wills.

DID YOU KNOW?

Wills buried his diary of the expedition beneath the "Dig Tree"; it is our main source of information about the trip.

The transcontinental trip went from the coast of Victoria in the south to the Gulf of Carpentaria in the northwestern part of Queensland.

Wills, Burke, and John King buried a note beneath the "Dig Tree" where the supplies had been. But they left no sign for any rescuers they had been there.

The party left Melbourne in August 1860, with 24 camels and 28 horses. But Burke had planned poorly. He intended to take the fastest route, even if it meant missing vital water holes and food sources.

Disaster Looms

At Cooper Creek, Burke left a party behind while he, Wills, and two others made a dash for the north coast. It took four months to reach mangrove swamps at the edge of the Gulf of Carpentaria (the swamps stopped them reaching the sea itself). The men had crossed the continent. But they were short of food. One man, Charles Gray, died on the return trip to Cooper Creek.

COOPER CREEK

Burke, Wills, and John King returned to Cooper Creek 18 weeks after they set out. The others had left hours before, leaving food buried beneath the "Dig Tree." The three men set out southwest, so when a search party arrived at Cooper Creek there was no sign the three had been there. When they got back to Cooper Creek, Burke and Wills both died. King was rescued by Aborigines.

1844–1874

JOHN MCDOUALL STUART

Unlike some of his contemporaries, John McDouall Stuart was an accomplished explorer of the Australian interior. He was a trained surveyor and had years of experience exploring in Australia before he made his first transcontinental expedition. He had taken part in Sturt's 1844–1846 trip.

John McDouall Stuart was one of the most skilled explorers of Australia—but the desert conditions of the interior left him close to death.

Stuart's explorations in the 1850s helped to open the area around Spencer Gulf, on the Great Australian Bight in South Australia, for settlement.

DID YOU KNOW?

In 1860, Stuart discovered a mountain he thought was the center of Australia; it wasn't, but it is still named for him.

Stuart made two unsuccessful attempts to cross Australia on horseback. In 1860, his party reached Attack Creek before their supplies ran out. Early the following year, they got further but found their way blocked by dense scrubland.

Third Time Lucky

In October 1861, Stuart and his men finally found a route through the scrub. From there, they had a relatively easy journey across grassy plains. The 2,000-mile (3,200 km) journey ended at the sea. The return to Adelaide was hard. The trip left Stuart almost blind and crippled; he had to be carried on a stretcher between two horses.

JOHN FORREST

A native Australian, John Forrest explored the interior of Western Australia. In 1869, he led a party from Perth on a 2,000-mile (3,200 km) inland trip looking for fertile pastureland. He then made the first west-to-east crossing of Western Australia. He crossed central Western Australia in 1874. Later, he became Western Australia's first prime minister.

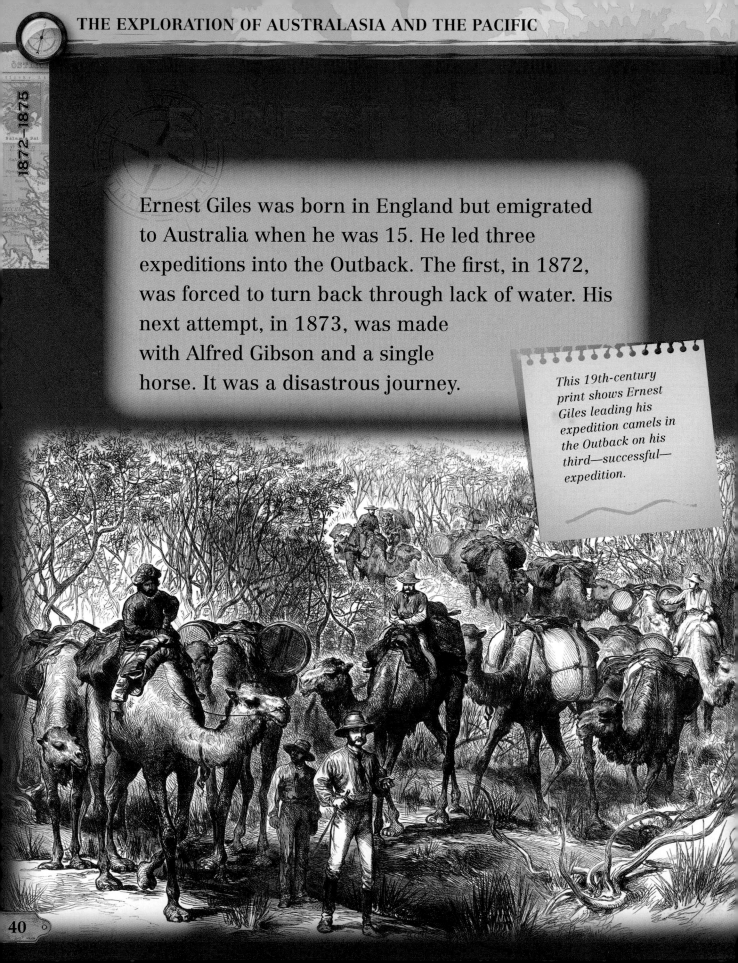

1872–1875

Ernest Giles was born in England but emigrated to Australia when he was 15. He led three expeditions into the Outback. The first, in 1872, was forced to turn back through lack of water. His next attempt, in 1873, was made with Alfred Gibson and a single horse. It was a disastrous journey.

This 19th-century print shows Ernest Giles leading his expedition camels in the Outback on his third—successful— expedition.

In the Outback, survival sometimes depended on finding the occasional water holes that were dotted around the dry landscape.

Searching for water in the desert, Giles and Gibson split up. Gibson was never seen again. Giles went crazy in the baking sun, but somehow survived.

Camels to the Rescue

For his final expedition, from May to November 1875, Giles used camels instead of horses. This time he successfully crossed the Great Victoria Desert as he traveled from South Australia to Western Australia. He had covered a total of 2,500 miles (4,000 km) across the heart of the continent.

DID YOU KNOW?

After Gibson disappeared, Giles traveled 450 miles (720 km) in the desert without finding water—but he survived!

WORKING CAMELS

Camels were often used for transportation in the deserts of South and Western Australia. The animals were first imported in the 1820s from India and Arabia. Camels can go for a month without water, can survive on poor food, and can carry heavy loads. That made them more useful than horses. Thousands of wild camels still roam the Outback.

1814–1848

NEW ZEALAND

New Zealand was the last major territory to be settled by Europeans. Polynesians had lived on the two islands since the 9th or 10th centuries. They called themselves "Maori." The first Europeans to arrive were sealers, whalers, and traders. In 1814, Christian missionaries arrived.

DID YOU KNOW?

The Maori never climbed New Zealand's highest peak, Aoraki or Mount Cook, because they believed it to be sacred.

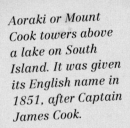

Aoraki or Mount Cook towers above a lake on South Island. It was given its English name in 1851, after Captain James Cook.

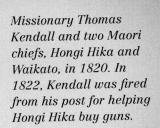

Missionary Thomas Kendall and two Maori chiefs, Hongi Hika and Waikato, in 1820. In 1822, Kendall was fired from his post for helping Hongi Hika buy guns.

Samuel Marsden was the first missionary. He arrived on North Island in 1814. Marsden and other missionaries tried to turn the Maori into Christians. Some later missionaries became explorers by accident as they tried to locate Maori to convert. One was William Colenso. He traveled through North Island in 1841 and 1842, collecting insects and plants.

South Island

On the less-populated South Island, the leading explorer was Thomas Brunner. He made three separate journeys with his trusted Maori guide, Kehu, between 1846 and 1848. He concluded that there was little worth exploring on the west coast. Today, the area still has few inhabitants.

THE MISSIONARIES

Samuel Marsden made sure that the missionaries he sent to New Zealand were practical men. They took their families and carpenters and other craftsmen so they could set up communities. They also introduced the Maori to Europen farming and business techniques and technology. In that way, Marsden hoped to show the Maori the superiority of European ways.

1831–1836

DARWIN AND THE BEAGLE

Darwin sailed on the Beagle at age 22, just after graduating. One of his roles was to keep Captain Robert Fitzroy company on the voyage.

The British naturalist Charles Darwin is best known for his theory of evolution. He developed his ideas about how life evolved while serving as a naturalist on a ship in the Pacific. He set out on the HMS *Beagle* in 1831. The voyage was meant to last two years. Instead, it turned into a five-year epic that changed history.

DID YOU KNOW?

The *Beagle* was a warship that had been converted to a surveying ship. Its captain was Robert Fitzroy.

The Galápagos are a group of 15 main islands and many small islets. Darwin found that species varied slightly between islands.

Darwin realized that finches on different islands in the Galápagos had different-shaped beaks that were adapted to eating particular sorts of food.

The *Beagle* sailed along the Atlantic and Pacific coastlines of South America. Darwin collected specimens of plants, animals, and fossils from everywhere he went ashore. The more he saw, the more he began to wonder about what caused the variations in the same species of animals that he saw in different environments.

An Epic Journey

After traveling up the Pacific coast of South America, the ship stopped at the Galápagos Islands. From there, it headed across the Pacific to New Zealand, via Tahiti. It then continued on to Australia and then to South Africa before it finally returned to England in October 1836.

GALÁPAGOS ISLANDS

The month Darwin spent exploring the islands of the Galápagos in 1865 was the most important of his whole journey. Why, he wondered, were species on the islands similar but different in detail, like the beaks of finches? He realized that, over time, species had adapted to their specific environment. From this observation grew Darwin's famous theory of evolution.

GLOSSARY

cape A headland that juts into the ocean.

chronometer A very accurate clock.

circumnavigation A voyage around something, such as an island or the whole globe.

colony A settlement founded in a new territory by people from another country.

continent A very large landmass.

expedition A journey made for a particular purpose.

latitude The position of a location on Earth's surface either north or south relative to the equator.

longitude The position of a location on Earth's surface either east or west relative to the Greenwich meridian.

maroon To leave someone in a place from which there is little chance of escape.

missionary A person who preaches in order to persuade other people to convert to a religion.

mutiny An uprising against officers in a military service, such as the navy.

naturalist A scientist who studies or collects plants and animals.

Outback Remote and usually uninhabited inland areas of Australia.

scurvy A disease caused by lack of vitamin C.

sextant A device used for navigation by measuring the height of the sun or other heavenly bodies.

strait A narrow channel connecting two much larger bodies of water.

survey To accurately measure an area of land.

tropical Related to the warm, moist belt around the globe on either side of the equator.